ORFF
Explorations

*Classroom projects in music,
movement and poetry*

ALICE BRASS

Illustrations by
NAZY SAKHAVARZ

ROBIN BRASS STUDIO

Reprinted by Robin Brass Studio Inc., 2012
www.rbstudiobooks.com

Printed and bound in Canada by Marquis Imprimeur, Cap-Saint-Ignace, Quebec

ISBN 13: 978-1-896941-34-9
ISBN 10: 1-896941-34-6

Cover: Based on design by Molly Brass
Illustrations: Nazy Sakhavarz

National Library of Canada Cataloguing in Publication

Brass, Alice, 1941-2003

Orff explorations : classroom projects in music, movement and poetry / Alice Brass ; illustrations by Nazy Sakhavarz.

ISBN 1-896941-34-6

1. School music – Instruction and study. 2. Music – Instruction and study – Juvenile. 3. Xylophone music – Teaching pieces. I. Sakhavarz, Nazy, 1972–
II. Title.

MT10.B824 2003   372.87'044   C2003-900965-3

Available from

In Canada: Chapters.Indigo.ca, McNallyRobinson.com, Amazon.ca, St. John's Music, Waterloo Music Company and other music retailers.

In the United States: West Music and Amazon.com.

Worldwide: McNallyRobinson.com.

Contents

ACKNOWLEDGMENTS

I would like to thank the children and the parents of the children at Claude Watson School for the Arts, an elementary school in the Toronto District School Board, for their inspiration and their enthusiasm, which has encouraged me to write this material.

Lois Birkenshaw-Fleming, author of many books on music for young children, has been a great support through my years at Claude Watson. She taught me to be free and creative with Orff and to allow and encourage the children to lead the way. For this I owe her much gratitude. She was very influential with my first book, *Orff Day by Day*. She has also read a draft of this book and her many suggestions were very helpful.

Thanks also to Dale Hyde, who has taught me about dance and children. He had a major part in preparing the lessons on dance in this book.

Ian Handscomb, artistic program director at Claude Watson, and Noam Markus, a teacher and professional mime, Assunta Colisimo, an art teacher, and Zoë Brass have assisted me with the original draft of this manuscript and offered helpful suggestions and support.

Thank you to my family, who listen to endless tales of the wonderful children I teach and have always encouraged me to continue.

Nazy Sakhavarz, who created the illustrations for my first book and for this one, has brought the book to life. I have known Nazy since she was a student at Claude Watson School for the Arts and have always admired her work. She is currently teaching and showing her magnificent oil paintings at a major gallery in Toronto, Ontario.

Alice Brass

Orff Planning Outlines

Music is a gift. Someone gave it to me. I am giving it to you so you can pass it on to others.

For those of you who have used *Orff Day by Day* this section is partially repeated as I still have the same ideas about Orff in the classroom.

My objective is to give teachers a plan of how to proceed through an Orff project using all the various Orff components of music, drama, language, movement and rhythm. I have concentrated on the form and structure of the music, assuming that other parts of the music program – good vocal technique, note reading, etc. – will be taught concurrently.

It is not necessary to complete every step of every project and teachers should read each set carefully, using only what works for them. All classes will react differently and as a teacher you need to be prepared to change your plans on the fly.

WHAT IS ORFF OR THE ORFF APPROACH?

The Orff approach allows children to explore how music is created and what role they can have in its creation. It encourages them to react to music, not only to the notes but to the form and the rhythm. This reaction is expressed by clapping, body percussion, chants, singing and/or playing instruments that Carl Orff designed to be very simple to use.

As in any art discipline, a certain amount of technical ability is essential before it is possible to be creative.

It is very important that children learn to sing, read notes and perhaps play a conventional instrument. The Orff approach is not intended to replace these skills but to enhance them. If you have only a short period of time each week to teach music, then your creative Orff approach will be combined with note reading, solfège, developing a good singing tone, etc. In this book, I have concentrated on the creative side of the projects.

It has also been my experience that an accomplished orchestral player can happily share an Orff class with children who cannot yet read music. Neither one of these participants is either bored or frustrated and both see the joy of music and of participation.

If you are new to the Orff approach, I encourage you to try it and, as well, to attend Orff workshops and courses to discover new material and ideas about how to use the children's ingenuity to make music fun for all.

THE CREATIVE PROCESS

When you are asking children to be creative and work in groups, you must be prepared for some noise and organized chaos. Children cannot be creative with drama and music in silence. You must let the children *play* a bit if you are to see the magic a child can bring to a situation.

Note: I try to limit this open creativity to ten minute stretches.

The younger the class the shorter the time they can focus on open-ended ideas such as "What can you do with this poem to tell the story?" I have them perform for each other long before their ideas are complete to keep reminding them of their tasks.

You will find that three or four children to a group is plenty. More than that and arguments get in the way of creativity. Once the ideas are firm the groups can often be amalgamated to create a more interesting production.

I have **some parameters** which I enforce to ensure some level of quality control.

1. "No sex or violence in Orff." By this I mean no mock fights, no bad language, and no bathroom jokes. The children sometimes argue and say that this is unrealistic but I am very firm and tell them "not in Orff". These ideas might be saved for older classes in drama.

2. Another rule is that each group must be able to perform something, usually at the end of each class. A lack of performance is not acceptable. There are excellent performances and good performances, and perhaps silly performances but **the only unacceptable performances are the ones that don't happen.**

A WORD ABOUT THE INSTRUMENTS

With each piece of music I have suggested what I think is essential and other elements that may be of interest. You should feel free to **use whichever of these suggestions work for your class.** The instrumentation is a suggestion but is certainly not the only way to do it. For instance I do not like using B flats and F sharps – because this often leads to misplacing the natural Fs and Bs. So wherever possible I change these notes in the accompaniment to some other note that will work. If this housekeeping problem is easy for you to manage, then these notes can be used very effectively.

The choice of instruments is definitely limited by your inventory as budgets are very tight for new equipment. If you are starting a new program and have a budget, you should probably start with two to four xylophones – some alto, some soprano; two to four glockenspiels – some alto, some soprano; one or two metallophones alto and/or soprano; hand drums, tambourine, wood blocks, bells and whistles for sound effects; a cymbal and any other percussion things you can find. I often buy equipment in toy stores and discount stores when I see something that would make a good sound.

You can make instruments for sound effects – shakers are easy, and a string through a hole in a tin can pulled on by a wet cloth makes a wonderful sound. The bigger the can the lower the sound. One-inch doweling cut into pieces one foot long can make rhythm sticks or lummi sticks.

A bass xylophone is a great addition to any Orff performance but these are expensive. Sometimes a parent group can be persuaded to help purchase such an instrument.

One of the projects in this book is putting together a piece with many parts, *The Orff Orchestra*. I have described as completely as possible how I would approach this as it is a question I have often been asked. If you feel overwhelmed by this type of project, perhaps this will help you. If you do not have at least eight melodic instruments of different timbres, this project is not for you.

Throughout this book, I have suggested certain instruments but you and the children should certainly experiment with these to try out different sounds.

If you have only three or four melodic instruments but many drums, bells, sticks, cymbals etc. you probably cannot tackle two of the projects in this book, *The Orff Orchestra* and *Exploring the Rhythm of Word Patterns*. All the rest can be done with very few melodic instruments.

TECHNICAL SKILLS

Some technical skills on the instruments are necessary before you can be creative. I would recommend many of the beginning pieces and exercises from *The Orff Schulwerk, Book 1* published by Schott. These develop handing technique, sound production, coordination and playing together in ensemble. I like to have every child in the class able to play every part. This is difficult to do when you have enough instruments for only six to eight students to play at a time. So since some of the parts are always easier than others, make sure that each student can play at least one part. Then they will be able to play for each other when it is time to be creative.

Orff, of course, uses a lot of rhythmic clapping exercises and patsching exercises to develop coordination and this is very useful but it still is not quite the same thing as hearing the sound the instrument makes.

SPACE FOR WORKING

When you start working on creativity, you need as much space as your school can allow. A gym is ideal. In my situation this space is rarely available. A large empty classroom is the next best space and extra hall space where the children can be supervised can help immensely. It is difficult to create sounds when you cannot hear what you are creating so groups need to be spread out. On the other hand, when creating a dance or a dramatic scene you do not require as much space.

If you have a regular classroom with desks that are hard to move, keep your groups small and direct projects with these constraints in mind. It is very frustrating for a child to try to be creative when space restrictions make the effort seem impossible.

USE OF TOYS

Whenever I am in a toy store or recreational setting, I am always on the lookout for noisemakers, animal sounds and interesting percussion items. They are not always of good quality and do not always survive the children's heavy hands but they are fun while they last. Bicycle horns are a good example – they often get used, but they do break.

Check your gym cupboard for hula hoops, balls, rings, skipping ropes, etc. These can often be used by children in ways you would not expect. Of course your supervision is essential but when such items are used wisely they can be very effective.

MATERIALS, MUSIC SOURCES

I am often asked what are the best sources of Orff music. There are, of course, many excellent books available and each classroom has its own needs.

When I was first introduced to Orff, I purchased many books at Orff workshops where music publishers displayed their wares. Having used many of these excellent sources, I keep returning to the *Orff Schulwerk* books, originated by Schott and now distributed by Warner Bros. There are five books in the series but I find Book 1 to be particularly useful. All of the others have material that is easily accessible to junior grades. In addition, the *American Orff Schulwerk* in three volumes has many wonderful creative ideas for all ages. Despite their titles, they work well across all grade levels. I have used the primary book for material for grade five and the book designed for junior grades as material for a primary class.

THE ORDER OF THE PROJECTS

The projects in this book are not in any particular order. Some use instruments and some do not. The sections can be tackled in any order that works with the rest of your program. You should feel free to change any of the material to suit your purposes. Pages have been provided at the beginning of each project for your own notes.

I have completed all of these projects and taken many of them to workshops and Orff conferences. If you have difficulty with any of them, I would be happy to discuss your concerns with you. My email is on the website listed at the back of this book and I am always happy to help where Orff is concerned.

In this book I have presented some of my ideas for exploring and integrating various forms of the arts – Dance, Drama, Poetry, Speech, Art – with Orff type presentations. I hope that some of my ideas will spark ideas of your own.

After I have provided the framework I rely on the children for their creativity. Let the children lead you, occasionally away from your intended goal. If you see value in their suggestions, follow their ideas.

You must, of course, first teach the techniques necessary for good instrument playing, good co-operation when working in groups and wise use of percussion instruments. Having done this, I view my role as that of a facilitator of their ideas.

In the education of any child, it is helpful if that child feels safe trying their own ideas in a controlled environment. In Orff, some ideas will naturally be more successful than others, but the biggest success of all comes from the way children learn from each other, for themselves.

Orff – Music and Movement and Fun

THE TEACHER MUST BE A MUSICIAN WHO IS INTERESTED IN MOVEMENT

The apparent simplicity of Orff is for the children only. While Orff is aimed at both musicians and non-musicians, the teacher must have a solid understanding of the structure of music.

Teachers using the Orff approach will benefit greatly from an interest in movement. Knowledge of the ways a body can move is helpful to guide students through their exploration. As well, an understanding of movement through time, space and the child's available energy is essential to guide students through this learning process. The children will do the moving but the teacher must be able to discuss their ideas, suggest alternatives and stretch their imaginations

This book incorporates one project written with the help of a dance teacher, Dale Hyde, who has helped me with many performances. I am hoping that this section will encourage non-dancers to try some simple movement and then perhaps be inspired to take some dance classes to help their teaching.

INTEGRATION OF THE ARTS AND ACADEMICS

The valuable process of integrating the various arts areas as well as bringing together arts and academics can be handled naturally through an Orff program. I have discovered that children love to interpret art with their own movement, to which they can add music they have cre-ated or music that is already part of the literature. The most exciting aspect of this type of integration is that it is often developed by the children themselves when they think they are playing and don't notice they are working.

SUITABLE AGE GROUPS TO ENJOY ORFF

Although Orff can be beneficial in almost any stage of a person's education, an ideal time to begin is around the age of eight. At this time, children are still relatively uninhibited about being creative in front of their peers, and yet they

have developed the skills necessary to take full advantage of Orff techniques. Many early childhood programs use Orff methods at younger ages and Orff can certainly add a great deal to this kind of program, but unfortunately many children leave Orff behind just at the age when it would be most useful.

ORFF IS FUN

With all the technical advantages of Orff set aside, it is fun for children and it shows no prejudice. Possessing great violin playing skills does not mean that combining a poem with sounds and movement will be boring. Likewise, the complete beginner at music will have just as much valuable input into a project as all the other students. In the words of a student, "Orff is instruments, it's moving, and it's fun!"

Orff is not about literal interpretation of music, or telling the children how it should be done. Orff is about how music makes the children feel and their insight into why it makes them feel that way.

What Is Your Name ?

You can use this as an introduction to the school year. It is a good way to learn names and meet new students.

Children enjoy using their own names and the names of their friends. They often do not realize that their own name has any rhythm nor have they thought about how many syllables make up their name. I have often used only the first three days of this project at the very beginning of Orff classes but return to it a year later to create the rhythmic pieces that are possible.

Creativity with the names increases as the children know each other better, so the whole project with names should probably be done after January or in a situation where the children know each other well.

Children find it quite magical when a whole piece of music can be made around their names and those of their friends.

Notes and Inspiration

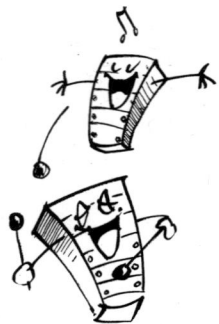

Names Have Rhythm

DAY ONE – RECOGNIZING THE SYLLABLES IN YOUR NAME

Ask the children to clap the rhythm of their own name

Obviously Bob, Dave, Sue, etc. are one clap.

Tommy, Alice, Mary, Cathy, Jimmy are also quite simple with a ti-ti rhythm beginning with the strong beat.

The difficulties come with Barbara, Melissa, Jonathan, Dorothy, etc. You will need to discuss where the strong beat falls. Do you say each syllable with the same emphasis? Obviously not, but the children have not often considered this.

Longer names like Jeremiah, Angelina, Marianna will also be discussed. You can demonstrate by saying these names in many different ways with the emphasis on different syllables and the students will quickly realize which one is right.

Once this seems clear to most, you can go on to add the last name, which is often quite a challenge especially in a class with many ethnic backgrounds.

Next choose 4 children to work out a pattern with their names. You might want to start with only first names. Suppose we have Jonathan, Mary, Cathy and Bob. One rhythm might be

> *Mary, Cathy, Jonathan, Bob.*

or

> *Jonathan, Mary, Cathy, Bob*

Encourage them to say this four times is a row and end with perhaps "yeah". Music works well ending on a strong beat so a single-syllable name works well as an ending.

Encourage the entire class in groups of 4 to try this. If you have uneven numbers make one or two smaller groups and have the children repeat one name to give the group the necessary four beats.

Assuming you have worked on clapping, snapping, patching, and stamping echo patterns, ask the children to make up some of these patterns to the rhythm of their names.

If you have never worked on this type of pattern, you could introduce this through the use of these name rhythms. I start many of my classes with several minutes of echo patterns of patching, clapping, snapping and stamping. It is then easy for the children to create their own to fit their newly created rhythms.

As always, end each class with group demonstrations of their work.

DAY TWO – STRETCHING THE PATTERNS TO INCLUDE LAST NAMES OR REPEATED FIRST NAMES

If necessary review the ideas of the rhythm of names. Now you could discuss stretching out these ideas to make a longer piece.

For example, using the same names

> *a) Bob and Mary, Bob and Mary, Cathy, Cathy Jonathan*

or

> *b) Jonathan, Jonathan, Jonathan, Jonathan,*
> *   Mary, Cathy, Bob – Heh!*

These could also be transferred to body percussion. I find if you encourage the children to stand instead of sitting they will add body movement (i.e. dance) without any encouragement. They will jump, turn, clap each other's hands etc.

Depending on your class, you can stretch this by adding last names, or give the students the choice of using last names or not.

Bob Smith, Jonathan Reilly, Cathy Tarczy-Jones

If some groups manage this easily while others are still working, you can ask these groups to create an introduction – either with words, rhythm or movement.

Be prepared! It will be very noisy but I think the result is well worth it. Children cannot be creative silently.

After ten to twelve minutes working on their own, ask to see some of the results. Some groups may need help and others will be amazing. Ask the students for their opinions. Talk about the compositions they have created.

This is as far as I would go with this project if this is the beginning of Orff and the children have no technical experience with percussion instruments.

DAY THREE – ADDING PERCUSSION INSTRUMENTS

Divide the children again into groups 4 to 6 to a group. (The smaller the group the less they argue.) Have them work on a name rhythm as on the previous days. Then give them some percussion instruments (you choose). Where possible, each child in the group should have a timbre different from the others. For example, if you have six children, you might give out one glockenspiel, one xylophone, one drum, one set of claves, one set of bells and one tambourine. Another group might have a totally different set of instruments. I would not expect a melody from the melodic instrument but rather a repeated rhythm pattern. You might suggest the notes for them to play – perhaps a fifth apart.

Encourage the children to use these instruments to play their rhythm. One way for the children to do this would be for each instrument to represent one name. They might also play two instruments together for two names, either playing simultaneously or one following the other, and then repeat this rhythm several times.

As you see them working at this, some may be ready to put an introduction to their creation. After about 10 minutes stop them, listen to what they have created, discuss it and have them try again. I expect you will be quite surprised at their creativity.

DAY FOUR – SIMILAR TIMBRE INSTRUMENTS WITHIN A GROUP

Working with the same idea, this time give out the instruments with similar timbre within a group. For example a glockenspiel, bells, triangle, cow bell to one group while another would have a xylophone, claves, maracas, lummi sticks, etc. Yet another group could have many different sizes of drums. Again let them work at creating rhythms with their name patterns.

By now you may find the students expanding the use of the names – repetitions, last names, pauses, echoes, etc.

DAY FIVE – CREATING MOVEMENT WITH BIGGER GROUPS

Tip: This is probably quite easy for you to do if you are trained in movement. If dance is foreign to you, here are some suggestions before you start on this activity.

Talk to the whole class about one of the rhythms:

e.g. Mary, Mary, Cecilia, Cecilia, Jonathan, Jonathan, Bob

Clap the rhythm, stamp the rhythm. Now walk the rhythm with the feet. Would skipping or hopping work with this? Could you swing a partner? How could you move differently for "Bob" because it is only one syllable?

Join two groups together and ask one to play their rhythm while the second group creates some form of movement that goes with the rhythm.

Have the groups switch roles so that by the end of the class you have two movement pieces from each of the groups.

You will have had to decide at the beginning of the class whether they are using mixed-timbre instruments or similar-timbre instruments as we used on Day Four.

DAY SIX

You might want to improve Day Five, but if this is complete and there are some good interpretations of the rhythm patterns, you can go on.

We need to create a joining section so that we can make a complete presentation of our class of names.

This can be done with a unison clapping pattern, or some similar pattern on the percussion instruments. Alternatively if you have poets in your class you might want to try two lines of verse; e.g.:

Names, names, what's a name?
You know who we are!

The class can once again be divided into small groups to create a pattern that they think would be appropriate. After about 10 minutes these can be tried and the best one chosen, or if one is not yet done, listen to what has been accomplished, encourage the best of the group and try again for a short period of time.

DAY SEVEN

Try the whole thing together, the rhythm patterns with names, and percussion instrument from each set of two. Use the unison pattern established on Day Six in between each group presentation. You now have a Rondo ABACADA, with the A being the unison pattern and B, C, D being the created rhythms.

Discuss with the students how they could improve this rondo. The order of presentation could be important.

They might want to change the instruments that are being used in certain situations.

The manner of joining the many sections might be discussed.

DAY EIGHT

A presentation to another class.

Reading Symbols

Orff and Music Reading Readiness

Reading music and following its instructions on an instrument is very much an exercise in remote control activities. In a way it is like using a computer, where you do one thing on a keyboard and see another thing on the screen. Interestingly, many musicians are very good at using computers.

Some children fall into these activities very easily and others seem to have difficulty. Some of the difficulty is simply reading the notes from the lines and spaces – I have found magnification sometimes helps greatly. But some children need help in learning to follow sequential instructions from printed material. In fact, it seems that learning to read music sometimes helps children learn to read words and thus follow other types of instructions.

Notes and Inspiration

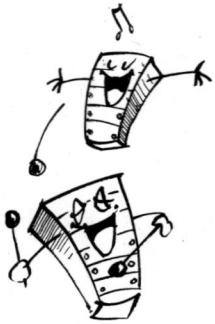

Starting to Read Symbols

DAY ONE – RELATING A SOUND TO A SHAPE

On the blackboard draw four different shapes such as a square, a circle, three parallel straight lines and a very long oval (long to distinguish it easily from the circle).

If you have sufficient instruments, give drums to some children, wood blocks or lummi sticks to some, cymbals, cowbells, etc. to some, and shakers or tambourines to the fourth group. You now have four sounds:

> *Skin sounds*
> *Wood sounds*
> *Metal sounds*
> *Clattering sounds*.

Each one of these sounds should respond to one particular shape. For example

> *The circle for the skins*
> *The square for the woods*
> *The long oval for the metals*
> *The parallel lines for the clattering shakers*.

Make a simple pattern of the sounds on the board:

e.g., Square, Circle, Square, Circle, Lines, Lines, Oval, Oval

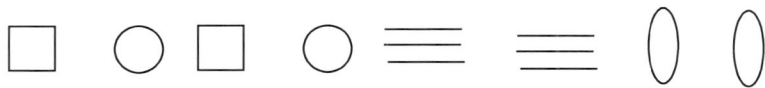

Ask the students to play their instrument as you point to the shape that applies to them.

Depending on the age of the children, this may happen correctly the first time or not until the fifth or sixth time. If you have only enough instruments for 10 children, then you will now have to switch children and try again.

When they can all do this easily, then you can do one of two things:

1. You can change which shape applies to which instrument, or
2. You can change the instrument which each child is playing.

When all this seems easy, you can add three more lines of shape instructions and try to play completely through it. From my experience some children will lose a bit of concentration and it will take several tries to get through it correctly.

DAY TWO – TWO SOUNDS AT ONCE

Using the same shapes and the same instruments you can write the instructions so that two instruments are playing at the same time.

The top line is for the circles and squares and the bottom line is for the lines and ovals.

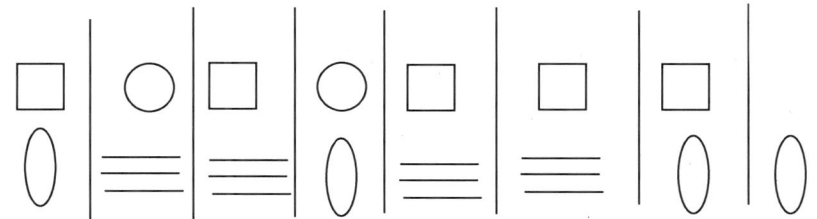

Ask the children for their input to create the next three lines of two-part music.

You might want to insert some rests in the middle of the lines at different times or indeed at the same time for absolute silence for one beat.

Once again, be sure that each child has a chance to play and that the instruments and instructions are changed.

These four lines of playing in two parts represent a piece of music that they have composed. Once you have something that sounds complete and that the children like, create an introduction or an ending using perhaps rhythm only or a verse or a crash of a cymbal – some way to start and end.

DAY THREE – DRAWING THEIR OWN SHAPES AND PATTERNS

Divide the children into groups of at least 4 and provide each group with one of each type of sound. Give out paper and pencils or markers or whatever you have and ask them to make their own diagrams of their sound patterns. Start out with only one color of marker or pencil so color does not enter into the composition.

Then ask them to practice their compositions and present them to the class.

If there is still time, switch compositions amongst groups and ask the students to play the composition of another group.

DAY FOUR – ADDING COLOR TO THE SHAPES AND THE MUSIC

Experiment with making the symbols graph visually interesting while creating the sound graph. Use different colored pencils or markers to indicate volume or intensity. This can become almost an art-music class similar to the discussion of *Orff, Shapes and Colors* on page 43.

Again play the compositions following the color instructions as well as the shape instructions.

DAY FIVE – MANY PARTS, LONGER PATTERNS

You can create a grid with more than 4 shapes thus breaking down your instruments into more sections.

Example:

> *big drums and small drums;*
> *wood blocks and rhythm sticks;*
> *tambourines and bells;*
> *cowbell and cymbal.*

In this case you have eight shapes and you can make eight lines of music to be played simultaneously. If you set this out in 12 beats and repeat it over and over, it can be very intense and quite fun to try.

Each horizontal line is one instrument as before and each space between the vertical lines is one beat. A blank space signifies a rest.

You should be the first conductor, pointing to the beats as they are played. Later the children can take turns in conducting.

Example:

I have given you one example here to illustrate my instructions but it is only one of many hundreds of possibilities.

Ask for the children's input as to how this would work and how it should be created.

DAY SIX

If your children can work easily in big groups divide them into groups of 8 or 10 and again give them a piece of paper to create their own 12-beat pattern. They will probably need a conductor to point to the beats and keep everyone in time.

This 12-beat type of rhythm is usually exciting to play and this is even greater if each group plays their piece at least 4 times through. An introduction and an ending can be added to make a complete composition.

The result of all this is that the children have written down their own composition and then followed their own instructions.

This will probably make following other types of written musical instructions – e.g. notation, guitar charts, etc. – an easier concept to grasp.

Poetry Has Rhythm

Martha studied her tables
Backward and forward, too,
But she couldn't remember six times nine
And she did not know what to do.

The teacher suggested she think of a friend
And not to bother her head.
"If you call the friend 'fifty four' for a while
 You'll learn it by heart instead".

Her favorite friend was Mary Ann
(Though she thought 'twas a dreadful shame
To call such a perfectly lovely friend
Such a perfectly horrid name).

She called her "my dear little 'fifty-four' "
A hundred times till she knew
The answer of six times nine as well
As the answer of two times two.

Next day Elizabeth Wigglesworth,
Who always acted so proud,
Said "six times nine is fifty two!"
Martha nearly laughed aloud.

But she wished she hadn't when the teacher said
"Now, Martha, tell if you can,"
For she thought of her friend and, sakes alive,
She answered "Mary Ann."

*Adapted from a poem
by Anna Maria Pratt.*

Notes and Inspiration

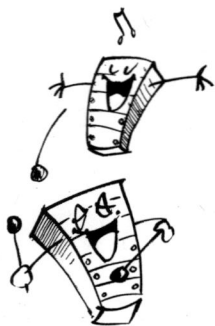

Poetry and Rhythm

This poem has wonderful scans, excellent rhythm and a little math for good measure.

Tip: A poem with simpler rhythms would be better for a younger group. The language skills definitely come into play here – so you have to know your class.

DAY ONE – THE BASIC BEAT

With a poem of this length I would always type out the poem and give a copy to each child for discussion. In the end the children will have the poem memorized but only because of frequent use.

The sentiment of this poem is not lost on children and so explanations and introductions are quite straightforward.

First you should say the poem to the class in at least two different ways, e.g., a 2/4 rhythm or a 6/8 rhythm. I have shown the first line scanned both ways as a sample. The children can choose whichever way works best for them but they should know there is a difference.

Ask one student or a group to clap the basic underlying beat while the class says the poem. This might take more than one attempt as they try to fit the words into the basic beat. Some discussion of the strong beat of each line may come into this. Some verses have a pickup, others start on the strong beat.

Now, have the whole class say the poem while everyone is clapping the beat. This will take a few tries to get the scan correct.

Next, talk about a different short rhythm or ostinato that could be played over and over to compliment the basic beat and go with the poem. Try some of these while discussing what works best.

2/4 — Mar-tha stud-ied her tab-les. Back-ward and for-ward too. But she

6/8 — Mar-tha stud-ied her tab-les, Back-ward and for-ward too. But she

Then have them work in groups of three, one saying one verse of the poem, another clapping the basic beat and the third clapping the slightly different ostinato – a contrast with the basic beat. This can produce some very interesting results but be prepared for some difficulties. The first time I did this, I wrongly expected it to be easy for all the students.

DAY TWO – TRANSFER TO PERCUSSION INSTRUMENTS

Again, hand out copies of the poem and divide the children into groups of three – two to play the beats and one to say the poem. Give each group two percussion instruments, e.g., woodblock and drum or tambourine and bell or whatever you have that will make contrasting sounds. You can use tuned percussion instruments if you do not have enough untuned ones. You can also use found sounds like desks, keys, etc.

Some children may find the basic beat more appealing if played only on the off beat but this makes it hard for the person saying the poem. They must work together for this.

For students who pick this up quickly you could challenge them to make an introduction and an ending while the others are still practicing and working at getting one verse together.

Have presentations from every group and be prepared to help some of the groups get their creations in sync.

DAY THREE – PLAYING THE RHYTHM OF THE WORDS INSTEAD OF THE BEAT

Now it is time to work on the word rhythm of each of the lines. We are trying to tell the story not so much in melody as in spirit and rhythm. Children often do understand the difference between rhythm and beat and this is a good chance to discuss this.

Starting with the whole class, clap the rhythm of at least the first verse. Talk about the difference between the beat we did on the previous day and the rhythm of each of the lines. (The children I was working with found this far more difficult than I had expected.)

Now have some students play this rhythm on two or three notes of the melodic instruments. We are not trying to create melodies here as we do when we improvise but rather to make a recognizable rhythm of the words of the poem when the rhythm is played. I used the melodic instruments only for contrast. You should choose what works best with your equipment.

Divide the children into groups of two or three to an instrument to create the rhythmic pattern of the verses. For variety assign different verses to each group. Be prepared to discuss their presentations. I would not expect them all to be right the first time.

DAY FOUR – DIFFERENT PATTERNS FOR DIFFERENT VERSES

Once they can play the rhythm of the words easily they might want to punctuate the sound with important words from each verse. For example "fifty-two" in verse five might be played a bit differently from the other words. Discuss which words are important and then let the children try again with their rhythmic patterns.

Again in groups of two or three, try to create inventive rhythm patterns that show off the word patterns as opposed to the ostinato from Day Two. I would assign one verse to each group. If it seems wise, you could give each group one untuned percussion instrument to accent the necessary words.

Again, listen to the groups perform and if possible play the whole poem through using all the groups.

DAY FIVE AND DAY SIX – THE OSTINATO AND THE RHYTHM TOGETHER

Now in groups of 4 or 5 put together the ostinato with the rhythmic interpretation. I found it was necessary to do quite a bit of review of the ostinatos versus the rhythm before getting started.

Choose the instruments carefully for each group. You should probably have some input into the mix of instruments for each group – children often choose an instrument by its appearance rather than its sound. Where possible, let the children experiment to see which effects they like the best. I assigned one verse to each group for a start.

So, one student will play the rhythm of the poem while saying the words. Another, will play the basic beat and a third and perhaps more will enhance the basic beat with an ostinato. This must all happen in coordinated time. In some groups that I watched one student chose to be the conductor and it seemed to help the end result.

These rhythm patterns can be presented and discussion take place around the better aspects of each.

My experience with this was that the children found it challenging to keep the whole thing in time – the poem, the rhythmic playing and the ostinatos. This is a very worthwhile exercise but do not become disappointed if the children find it difficult. Take an extra day to make it work.

Tip: Children often must be shown that two percussion instruments must have different timbres if their rhythms are to be differentiated, i.e. do not have two drums when you could have one drum and one tambourine; a cowbell and a cymbal do not give a good contrast; etc.

DAY SEVEN – SUGGESTIONS FOR FURTHER EXPLORATIONS

You could do each verse on its own with an ostinato to join the verses. The students can create an ostinato to join the verses together. One of the groups of children I was working with created a combination of a snappy beat on a wood block followed by "No, no, no Martha" to go between each verse.

If the children are trying to create a presentation, they need to be able to present the poem, its words and its rhythms without having one drown out the other. Hence the choice of instruments is important

In what order do you want to present the work? You could say the poem in choral fashion and then play your creation on the instruments. Alternatively, you could have one student recite the entire poem and then start their creations. Do you want the sound to follow each verse or accompany it? Ask the children for their input.

You could add some drama to the presentation to tell the story of the poem even better. This could add at least one more day this project and be used as a presentation for parents or other classes.

The Orff Orchestra

Many Interwoven Parts

An orchestra signifies many parts playing at the same time with interwoven melodies and rhythms. This requires technical skills for playing each instrument, complete knowledge of the parts and concentration in ensemble playing.

Tip: This is obviously not the project for the first day of your Orff classes. I teach grades four and five and the children have one hour of Orff a week. I do not try this until the very end of grade four or perhaps the beginning of grade five depending on the class.

Many teachers have expressed their anxiety over trying anything but the simplest patterns. I hope this will encourage you to try more complicated music.

First, I have the children sitting in what I call an Orff orchestra, as opposed to a circle used for improvisation (*see illustration, page 35*). In other words, glockenspiels near the front, then soprano and alto xylophones. Behind them metallophones and if you are lucky enough to have a bass, it should be at the back. Place untuned percussion along the side wherever it fits in your room, but all non-tuned percussion should be together. If you have recorder players they should all be together somewhere close to the front.

When I am teaching a piece that will eventually become a dance or a drama, I do not try to incorporate note reading as part of the lesson. I teach the whole piece by rote and by ear. There are some who would disagree with this approach but I find that playing by ear is just as important as playing from written notes. Sometimes the children who have already achieved very high note reading skills through private lessons on piano or violin actually have a bit of difficulty playing from verbal instructions and learning the melody and parts by ear.

I will assume for this project that you have 10 melodic instruments for 30 children and follow the lessons through in that manner. (Obviously a melodic instrument for every child in the class is ideal but seldom achieved in a regular school.) This piece of music has quite a lot of untuned percussion with challenging rhythms. The purpose of this is that even with only a few melodic instruments the whole class may be involved in the final performance.

Notes and Inspiration

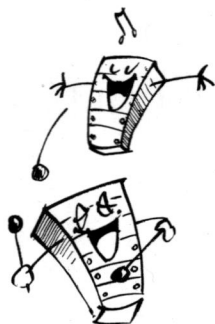

Learning Many Parts

Day One – Learn the melody

Begin by learning to sing the melody of the first eight bars to "la" or "loo". Work on the first eight bars until this is easy to sing. It is in the dorian mode so it is easy to sing the intervals.

Have the children divide into groups of 3, each group with a melodic instrument. Using their fingers on the notes say the note names while placing one finger from each hand on alternate notes, i.e, A D C D A D C A G F G F E D. You know from your Orff training that it is important to use two hands always and alternate them note for note.

Tip: Start with fingers instead of beaters so that the children farthest away from you can hear your voice.

Make sure they are all in the right octave – starting on the lowest "A" on each instrument. Do this very slowly once. Then divide the exercise and work only on the A D C D A D C over and over again until it is easy. Try this with mallets. Switch to another member of each group, who will probably learn faster than the first group simply from watching, and then when this is accomplished switch again. This way, all the students will learn the melody.

Follow the same pattern with the A G F G F E D. Maybe this time start with the third group and work backwards towards the first group. Make sure they see the *pattern* of the notes – i.e. A G F G F E D – is straight down then back up one and down again to D. As with everything, some will learn this very easily and some will have difficulty.

Now, starting with the second group of students, try both parts of the melody together one after the other. Try it first using fingers so you can call out the notes and they will be able to hear you. By the end of the first class everyone should be able to play the melody for the first eight bars. You can ask for solos or group performances or whatever works in your class.

You could certainly at this point have a single student play the D A of the ostinato with the melodic performances. If you have a bass use it here. If not use an alto xylophone.

Day Two – Work on the underlying ostinato

The notes for this part suggested for the alto xylophone are easy to play but the rhythm can be challenging.

You can introduce a word rhythm that works with the given rhythm. Practice clapping before playing.

Example:

I'm happy "sniff" Yeh! "sniff" Yeh!

"sniff" is a place holder and seems to work well – the children are often amused. If sniff if too silly for your class try playing in the air for the rest.

If time permits, ask the children for their input on word patterns to hold the rhythm.

Hello, My First Name is Joe ! Yeh!

Rhythmic Section

Note: The name of this piece is played out by the last line of the rhythmic section. I find it much easier to teach odd rhythms using word patterns rather than counting.

The entire class can patsch on their knees the rhythm, with the rests being a motion out to the side to hold the space for the rest.

Again, in groups of three to an instrument all the children should learn to play this.

Tip: Make sure that in using the beaters or mallets, they pull the sound out of the bars to get a clear sound. If they hit the mallets into the bars they will get a dull thud. A simple demonstration usually solves this.

This alto xylophone ostinato can be learned and played on all the instruments at once. As soon as this is easy, have someone accompany this new ostinato with the D A ostinato from the bass line. Take note that in the first bar the two ostinatos are together but in the second bar they are on alternate half beats. Here the bass holds the place of the "sniff". Often this helps some children who have been struggling with the syncopated rhythm.

If you have extra time experiment with this rhythm, playing first one type of instrument then another. Try a canon where one starts one bar ahead of another. Anything that allows the children to feel comfortable with the rhythm is a good thing.

Day Three — Try all three parts together

You will probably have to review the melody from the first day before you begin. Switch the instrumental parts around. Start with the glocks playing the melody, the xylophones the rhythm and the bass or metallophone playing the D A. Then try with the soprano xylophones on the melody and the glocks and alto xylophones on the rhythm section.

Also, you could try dividing the melodic section into two parts – question from the first four bars and answer from the last four – glocks on the question and xylophones on the answer. Ask the children which combination they like best and why.

Now it is time to learn the next eight bars or section B

Try it like this. First, singing down the octave, sing the top line as a melody. The pattern is easy to learn and to play. I would have this part on the soprano metallophones. Then show them how the other part has the same musical shape down a fourth. I would put this on the alto metallophones.

(Alternative suggestion: Play the melody with the right hand alone Once this is easy, learn the next four bars in a similar fashion ending on A A instead of A D. Work this through all three members of each group using all the instruments as we did on Day One and Day Two To learn the harmony using fingers place right hand on A and left hand on E . Play the above melody with the right hand and shadow the motion with the left – i.e. down, down, down down, up up up down, etc. Most children find this easy to do once they have learned the first melody. Note that you can do this only on the alto instruments as the SX and SM do not have the high A and high G.)

Try playing the first eight bars (the A section), followed by the melody of the second eight bars (the B section). Do not yet add the other two parts to the B section but rather let the children hear the difference in timbre between the two sections. I would tend to have the melody of the A section on the soprano xylophone and the melody of the B section on the metallophone but you should try different groupings to see what you like best depending on your desired final result. Hard beaters on the metallophones can help to bring out the melody of this section.

Try this many times so everyone gets a chance to play.

DAY FOUR – LEARN THE REMAINDER OF THE B SECTION

You will notice that the bass rhythm for the B section is the same as the rhythm for the AX ostinato of the A section.

Since this rhythm is already well known, have a student play it on D, preferably on the bass xylophone. If you have no bass use an alto xylophone for the part.

Always choose from among your strongest musicians for the lowest part. In my classes the students can choose any instrument they wish except the bass. I reserve the right to choose the bass player. If the bass player is solid on the rhythm, it makes the rest of the piece much easier to play.

The third part in this second section, D E D C is easy to learn. Have everyone learn this and then try it using different instruments while playing the metallophone part from the melody. I chose to play this on glockenspiels so the melody would sound over the ostinato.

Having decided on the instrumentation, try all three parts of the second eight bars together. Since I assume the children are still in groups of three they should all try playing this new music.

Try together everything learned so far. If time permits try the music learned on Day One and Two, the A section with this new section B and then repeat the A section, an ABA form.

I think you will find the music moves along well and the children enjoy the sounds of the various parts.

DAY FIVE – THE RHYTHM SECTION

One of the rhythms of the first four bars of the rhythmic section is the same as one of the ostinatos in the first eight bars of the music. Therefore this will be easy to learn.

You can choose your own percussion instruments depending on availability. Let the children experiment with different combinations and choose one or two that seem to work well.

For example:

- *the top line might be a tambourine, the second line wood-blocks and the third line a hand drum.*
- *the second section of four bars might be played on the hand drum or a bongo drum would work well and be easy to play.*
- *the bottom system of these eight bars could be a combination of drum and tambourine, drum and wood block, two different timbre woodblocks, etc.*

Experiment with different sounds and ask the children for their input. They often come up with very non-conventional but eventually interesting combinations.

If time permits, you might want to try the whole piece to this point. Switch around the instruments and try again.

Day Six — The last line of rhythmic section

This rhythm is the basis for the name of the piece. It starts with a sniff.

"sniff" Hel-lo, my first name is Joe! Yeh!

I have written this for 12 bars – you can double it if it suits your purposes. Again, the choice of instruments is yours and your children's. My suggestion is to use all the percussion instruments for this part. It seems most effective to end with a straight eighth note rhythm probably on a drum to lead back to the A section.

Now you should try the whole piece – probably every child will now have an instrument to play. If you are still short of instruments, double some of the parts with clapping and stamping so that everyone can be involved in the performance.

Whenever I have taught this piece, the almost immediate reaction is "Can we play this for our classroom teacher?" It seems to have tremendous drive and energy and the children love to perform it.

Day Seven — Practice and presentation

Practice and perfect the piece and experiment with the various instrumental parts, allowing different children to try the various sections and instruments.

Alternative approaches

This is the end of learning this music. You can of course go on and create a dance to go with this. Lummi sticks make an excellent addition to this piece.

The first eight bars of melody make a very easy-to-play recorder piece. It could be played on the recorder perhaps the first time and then repeated on the glockenspiels or whatever you have chosen.

Using Your Feet To Tell the Story

The first time I saw this done was by a professional dancer in the Fringe Festival in Toronto. It was so intriguing that I tried it first with a class and then with a performance group. Each time it was very successful.

The children can express sentiment through body language only, specifically the feet. They already do this quite successfully when they stamp their feet in anger. But many other sentiments can be expressed this way and they have great fun trying it out. It may take a couple of tries before they all get the idea but the results are always interesting. This is also one project you can do with very few melodic instruments.

Notes and Inspiration

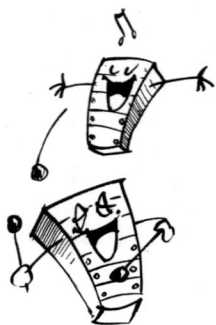

Rhythms of My Feet

DAY ONE – DISCUSS THE CONCEPT

Talk about the concept of using your feet for showing emotions. How could you show fear, excitement, worry, sadness, happiness, anticipation. For example, fear can be very slow careful steps with pauses. Excitement can be fast and perhaps experienced in place. Worry is different from fear so it might be slow but also in place. Anticipation could be several steps and then big pauses. These are only suggestions but I am sure the class can help you with ideas. Children often stamp their feet when they are angry so they will understand the idea of expressing emotion with their feet.

In groups of two or three, work out one emotion from each group, then show the results to the rest of the class and try to guess what emotion was being created. Ask for suggestions as to changes that could make the feet movements more descriptive.

If there is time, change groups and ask for a different emotion from the groups.

DAY TWO – CONSIDER VARIOUS SCENES OR STORIES

Discuss various little stories that could be told using the rhythm of feet. Some suggestions are various sports moves – baseball – strikeout and home run; a tennis game – perhaps with an audience; a gymnastic display with success and failure; in another vein, shopping in a crowded mall; teaching a class a physical skill – such as a dance or a sports move. One of the most successful that I saw was meeting and making new friends. Friends seemed not to be able to communicate until they could each understand and repeat the rhythm of the other friends.

Ask for some demonstrations of how some of this could work. The emotions dealt with on Day One will be part of each little story.

Once again, work in groups of three or four. Let the children choose the story or scene that appeals to them and have them work out the story with no words at all. The feet will express the "no I cannot" or " no I will not" or "hurrah, I have managed," etc. There can be some arm gestures such as holding the baseball bat but absolutely no speaking.

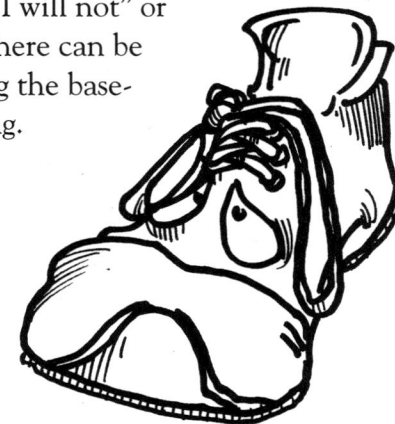

Day Three — Work out some examples

Talk about the actions of the day before. You want to encourage them to expand their story.

Here is an example. I am describing this because you may not have had the advantage I had in seeing professional dancers work these things out. I personally would not relate this example to the students but use it as a background for helping them to set out their own idea.

"Meeting and making new friends" started out as a simple rhythm from one person able to be copied by another person which then allowed them to work together.

This became expanded into three people doing the same rhythm with their feet, a sort of tap dance, as they walked down the street. They met someone else who wanted badly to join them. She tried various rhythms with her feet but the three would not pay any attention. Finally one of the group tried to teach her their rhythm but try as she might she could not get it right, so they went on their way. However, she kept practicing this rhythm and then all of a sudden she mastered it. She sought out the original three, and when she was able to join in exactly with them they went on their way together. It was as if the they were speaking the same language at last.

Another good example was a dance class where the students were anything but cooperative.

A dance teacher, one of the students, was trying to show the class the routine but the class seemed more interested in entertaining each other than in doing the steps. Eventually the teacher fainted and the students were quite upset. They realized their actions had really been hard on the teacher, so they tried to learn the routine on their own. When eventually the teacher was revived, the entire class was doing the routine, which delighted the teacher and they all danced away together.

These examples are for you to see the possibilities. Whether you want to give your students all this information depends on how much input they need to be creative. I sometimes find if I give them too much, they use my ideas instead of creating their own.

Once again, work in groups to try to create an actual scene combining all the emotions worked on the first day.

Showing and discussing the work of each group at the end of the class is again very important.

Days Four and Five — Expanding the scenes and adding sound effects

Again, expand the scenes created before. Encourage introductions and conclusions. Perhaps two groups could work together depending on what has evolved. I get very different results every time I try this. It depends largely on the interests of the particular group of children and also on how well they work together.

Every day should start with a discussion of what was developed on a previous day and end with a demonstration to the class of what has been accomplished.

This process of creating these scenes can take one to ten classes depending on your direction and your goals. The longer the children work on it the more intricate the rhythms and stories become. Only you know the tolerance of your class to perfect their work.

All of the scenes will be enhanced with percussion sound effects either from instruments or body percussion. Use these freely at this point. Just absolutely no words.

Day Six — The "A" part for the rondo

It is fun to join together the different scenes as it makes for a more complete project. This "A" section (joining section) can come after Day Three if it seems more appropriate for your situation.

This section can be many things;

- *a clapping stamping rhythmic pattern to be done by the whole class or a large group*
- *a rap verse*
- *a song*

I have given you a very simple example.

(*Tip: The* Orff Schulwerk Book One *is filled with such examples. This book is a wonderful resource. Here is a chance to teach one of the many rhythm patterns and then use it to enhance a performance.*)

You can teach a rhythm like this using tas and titis as follows:

ta rest ta rest titi titi ta heh (with hands)

titi ta titi ta rest ta ta rest (with feet)

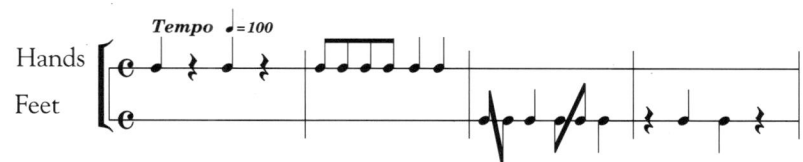

Note: Tails up right foot, tails down left foot.

Alternatively or simultaneously you can teach the hands part with a word rhythm such as:

Schools (rest) Out (rest) In the month of June Yeh!

The feet you could use:

Very soon, very soon, "sniff", at last, "sniff"

(The sniff is to hold the rest place. The final sniff is probably unnecessary)

One performance where the children used the feet rhythms for story telling was joined together by them pretending to change television stations with a remote control. Their movement was accompanied by a clapping rhythm.

Tip: A word on teaching rhythm patterns. Any rhythm can be taught using a word rhythm. You will find the students learn the rhythm very quickly. If you are using this lesson to teach the mathematics of music timing and counting, then this is not the time to use word rhythms. But if you simply want a rhythm pattern to use in a class or for a performance or in fact to help improve coordination, word rhythms will speed up the learning process.

Once the class can handle your rhythm easily, then ask them for ideas on presenting the rhythm; e.g. with the whole class clapping and stamping, standing in a circle clapping each other's hands and stamping feet – perhaps the two rhythms must be done by two different groups or perhaps the children can do both rhythms at the same time.

Another idea would be that the basic rhythm could be part of the story, encouraging the other groups to tell their story.

DAY SEVEN

Put the whole thing together as a rondo – each story being the B, C, D section and the clapping section the A part.

I am sure you will have great fun with this. It is quite non-threatening and can produce very interesting class work with broad participation, as well as a good performance if that is your aim.

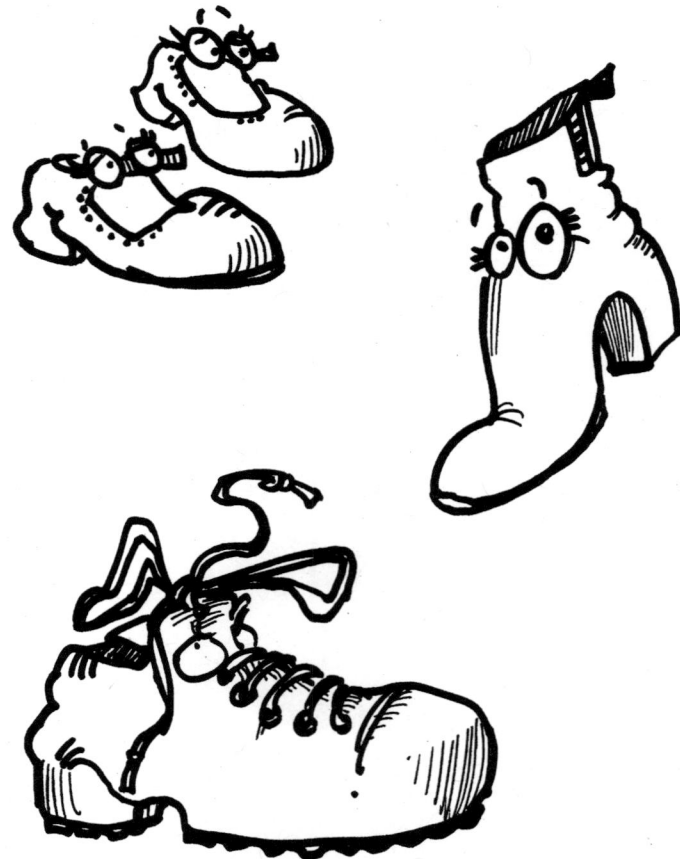

Orff, Shapes and Colors

Children love to interpret their art

Whenever I go to an art exhibition
It always has been my secret ambition
To act out the art
And sort of take part
Instead of just standing and looking

Children will look more carefully at art both in awe and critically if in some way they can participate in the art. For example, in making a picture of their own, if they are using the style of another artist as the prototype, they will do more interesting work if they are allowed to criticize as well as admire the work of the artist. In this way they can put their own artistic ideas to work.

This project combines Orff and designing with shapes. Combining videos and sound has become very commonplace for today's children so the idea of making soundscapes will be easy for them to understand. Hopefully this will be just the starting point from which you can combine other art projects with your music class.

Notes and Inspiration

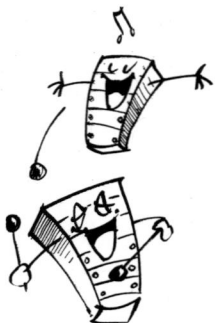

Interpreting Art

DAY ONE – SHAPES AND SOUNDS

Discuss the different sounds that various shapes might suggest. Draw them on paper or the blackboard.

A few examples to get you started:

- *many dots in a cluster* – *on a drum might be played with finger tips; on a glockenspiel random yet organized notes played in quick succession.*

- *a large circle* – *on a drum one beat; on a metallophone one long lasting stroke; on a cow bell one stroke.*

- *a straight line in an upward direction* *could be a glissando on any melodic instrument; or the wonderful sound that results from running a fingernail or damp cloth along a piece of string threaded through a hole in the end of an empty tin can and secured with a knot – the bigger the can, the deeper the note; etc.*

Have the children sit in a circle and give each child a piece of paper and a writing tool – a pencil, a felt tip pen or colored pencil – and one percussion instrument – melodic or non melodic. Ask them to draw one shape and be prepared to play its sound. Give them about a minute for this exercise. Now go around the circle while each child plays their shape.

Now have them pass their shape along the circle – I would recommend passing along to two people beyond but do whatever works for your children. Now after a minute for reflection the same pictures should be played again.

Talk about the differences and the effectiveness of the different instruments. Some shapes will have been very hard to do on another instrument and undoubtedly, some will be better.

If you have time change again.

Another variation, if there is still time, is to have two children sitting beside each other combine the sounds they have created for the two pictures.

DAY TWO – COMBINING SHAPES AND SOUNDS

Start with at least four students to a group and fresh paper. Ask the children to begin by drawing shapes that go together and would perhaps make a "cool" design. For the sake of a reasonable sound level in the classroom allow five to ten minutes of work without the instruments.

When some designs seem to take shape, distribute the instruments. I would take control over the mix of the instruments for each group but this would depend on your class. Two instruments per group is probably plenty given that each instrument can make a sound in many ways.

Ask the children to create a short soundscape around this design. It should probably be about four beats in length but repeated perhaps four times.

Then ask the children to use the same design but change the instrumentation within the group. Discuss the results.

Now pass the designs to a totally different group and everyone start again but with a different mix of design and sound.

Again discuss the results – i.e., which ones represent the design best and why it seems this way. Opinions will differ greatly but probably there will be consensus around a good combination of the design and the sound.

DAY THREE AND DAY FOUR – CREATING AN ENTIRE DESIGN

Now with six or eight to a group it is time to create a much more complicated and perhaps progressive design. By that I mean one that moves across the page – seeming to travel through itself. It might go in straight line, an upward diagonal, a downward diagonal, a swirl or itself move as if by random dots. The paper should be large to allow for several to work at once and inexpensive so that several starts can be made.

The color can start to make a difference to the interpretation – perhaps different sections repeated but in different colors. This could lead to a discussion of warm colors like red and orange and cool colors like blue and green and all the shades in between.

- **Cool colors** *could be softer; e.g. glockenspiel, triangle, finger cymbal – played very gently.*
- **Lighter colors** *could be softer; even drums can be soft.*
- **Warm colors** *could be louder and bigger like cow bells, big drums, large wooden instruments.*
- **Dark colors** *could be played perhaps by the lower instruments. This could take on a serious tone with drums, alto xylophone, bass, etc.*

Now we can add the instrumentation. The children must agree on how that should be done, co-operation being a large part of such an exercise. At this point each group might want to appoint a conductor to point to the different parts of the design that are being interpreted.

This whole process may well take two classes. I find that a number of short periods work well for the creative process for young children – up to grade 6. The children lose their concentration when working together for more than fifteen or twenty minutes. This, of course, will vary with the age of the children. Kindergarten creativity, I have discovered, lasts about one minute before silliness sets in.

DAY FIVE – MAKING A PRESENTATION

Your class could pin up all the designs in a row on the wall and play straight through them without a break. This is probably the simplest approach, so you could try this first and then ask for the reactions of the participants.

Perhaps there should be joining sections played between each set of designs. Here are some suggestions:

- **an ostinato** *created on one or a group of the instruments. This could be an instrumental section taken from Orff literature or it could be the students' own creation. If you decide on the latter, you will probably need at least one class for this creation.*
- **some simple movement** *between each design, i.e. presenting the picture with a flourish or walking or marching between the scenes with a simple accompaniment beat.*

- *a drama* about their creations – some might be sad, others thoughtful, some very happy. This will depend very much on the class, the other experiences they have had and their ability to work together.

- *poetry* you have been studying in English might work as a good way to join the art creations. (If this works for your class then you might want to introduce the poetry idea early and have the designs created around the poetry.)

Tip: The Orff Schulwerk, Book 1 *has many rhythmic ostinatos that would work well here. In my earlier book,* Orff Day by Day, *there are three projects directed at creating your own music and accompaniments.*

DAY SIX – A PRESENTATION

If you present this to another class you could start by asking the audience to listen to a soundscape and guess which design it represented. This, once again, allows the audience to participate in the performance. After everyone has had a good look at the various parts you could play the entire piece.

OTHER IDEAS FOR INTERPRETING ART

The art could also be made much more sophisticated by using the original designs done on proper art paper with paint or pastels. This is encouraged especially if you and/or your class has art skills.

One year the grade five students worked with specific paintings that had been done in art classes by grade eight students. Some of the soundscapes actually told the story of the painting. The older students were quite amazed at the interpretation of their work by the younger children. Of course when the pictures are more pictorial, this will encourage drama and sometimes a song known from some other source.

Another idea, if computers are available and easy to use, is to make the design creations on the computer. The repetitions can be very varied. You could use tangrams. The possibilities are many but the important thing is to interpret the visual with the sound.

So You Want to Teach a Folk Dance

This set of lessons will show that you can teach a folk dance even though you have little experience in this area. Most children enjoy participating in folk dances and you can use Orff music for the accompaniment. There is a lot of explanation in this lesson aimed at non-dancers. If you are a dancer, you can skim this part and try some of the suggestions or music or the dance set out after Day Three.

When I first started working with Orff methods I had no knowledge of how to teach dance. My good fortune in working at a school with an enriched arts program, where all the children have three hours of dance a week, brought me into contact with dance teachers and their methods.

I have often asked for help from these experts especially where performances were being prepared, and I have always been impressed at how quickly a trained dance teacher can change creative confusion into a dance.

I have had help with these lessons from Dale Hyde, a very experienced dance teacher who is comfortable working with young children and adults alike.

I hope this project will encourage you to try to teach a dance even if you have little confidence in this area. We have set out the basic technical needs for the dance and then we have described the form with the aid of diagrams.

In the diagrams, the circles are dancers and the little points are their noses to show which way they should face.

Good luck with this; we really would appreciate any feedback with difficulties you have following all these instructions.

Notes and Inspiration

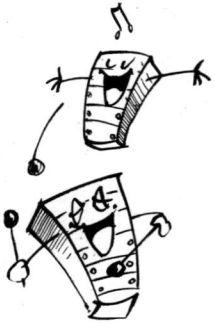

Let's Try This Dance

Children will sometimes object and say "I cannot dance" or something similar; if this is the case you may want to refer to this as moving to music or feeling the beat.

Tip: Holding hands is often part of the dance but not necessary to experiment with the form and rhythm. If the children object, work around this by simply not attempting to hold hands. However, this sometimes makes a dance more difficult. A possible solution can be drawn from the lumber camps. Folk dances helped to pass the time to fill in the long winter darkness, but of course there were no women, so they used handkerchiefs to simulate holding hands — each two grasped the same handkerchief. When hands needed to be held they would pull out a handkerchief and hand it to their partner.

DAY ONE – WALKING – THEY CAN ALL DO THIS.

Have one student beat the rhythm on the drum while the rest walk. Talk about the different meters in which you can walk:

- *1 2 1 2 – walk walk walk walk*
- *123 456 123 456 which is interpreted by dancers the same as 1 2 1 2 with one step for every three beats.*
- *1 2 3, 1 2 3 can be walk pause pause, walk pause pause*
- *1 2 3 4 is often danced as quick quick quick slow, or walk walk walk pause. Try walking these beats backwards and sideways as well as forward.*

Discuss a musical signal to tell the class to change direction; a very loud drum beat or a cowbell played by another student or perhaps a change of rhythm. Experiment with these things to see how well the students can respond to sounds while they are experimenting with their walking patterns.

If there is time, divide into groups with one person in each group playing the rhythm and perhaps a second playing the signal for change, while the rest create a walking pattern that lasts 16 or 32 beats. Give them 10 minutes to try this and then have them show you what they've done. Discuss what worked well.

DAY TWO – SKIPPING

Next we will try skipping. It is easier to demonstrate this than to explain it in words. If any of the children seem to have difficulty, pair them with someone who is good at it and soon all will be able to skip.

Ask the children to skip around the room while you play a rhythm on a percussion instrument. Having accomplished this, you might want to discuss what exactly they are doing and how it fits with the rhythm. They may be surprised how difficult it is to describe in words.

Try the patterns you were doing with the walking, i.e., changing directions; perhaps skipping backwards; skipping slowly with a pause and skipping quickly and constantly.

Using a rhythm pattern, combine the skipping and the walking, having the percussion instruments give the instructions, i.e. when to turn, when to change step, etc.

Now try it with partners and have the music instruct when to change partners. Ask the children for their input on the best way to give these instructions – drums, cowbells, tambourines, woodblocks, etc.

Once again have them work in groups to create a movement pattern using walking and skipping. To keep the noise level down I would give each group of four to six children only one percussion instrument. They will have to be creative in using the instrument to give their group instructions.

In doing this they are learning to listen to the music for the clues in creating the movement or dance.

DAY THREE — THE CHASSÉE

The children are ready to try a chassée. The following is a description of the step for those of you who are not dancers. Experienced dancers can skip this description and demonstrate the step for the children.

Chassée step (also called "slip" step, or "slide" step) is done in 2/4 or 6/8 time; *the same rhythm used for skipping.*

The easiest way for me, a non-dancer, to understand the step is as follows

> *To move to the right, step sideways on right, close left foot beside the right with the first step being on the strong beat.*

The one thing that must be added to this is that before the **first step** is a sort of hop on the foot that is opposite to the direction you intend to move. For example, if you mean to move right then you hop first on your left foot, then step on the right then slide the left foot to the right , step on the right etc. (A skip is very similar except you are moving forwards not sideways.)

The chassée begins by moving sideways right or left. The preparation is to have the body slightly elevated by supporting the weight on the balls of the feet and the heels are raised off the floor. All steps in the sequence are done on the balls of the feet (ideally, the heels never touch the floor).

In case you need to try this again, the following is another explanation of the same movement.

The step has four parts and the movement is to the right.

Introduction

- (count &) *To move to the right the weight is shifted slightly to the left foot and a small hop or lift is made with the left foot.*

Repeated Steps

- (count 1) *Step sideways to the right on the right foot.*
- (count &) *Close left foot beside right foot.*
- (count 2) *Step sideways to the right on the right foot*
- (count &) *Close left foot beside right foot.*

This can continue for as many steps as required.

Note: By using opposite footwork, the step will move to the left.

(Tip: As the teacher you can simply demonstrate this and not worry the children about the description.)

Once the students can do the chassée, experiment with different ways of using the step. One example is as follows:

Change Direction with the Chassée

Try challenging the children to change direction with the step. (This should always occur on the "&" or weak beat.) To do this assume we are moving right and that the weight is on the right foot; the next step will be the original lift hop on this same right foot followed by stepping on the left then sliding the right foot left, etc.

This will take a bit of practice and will be much easier if you can demonstrate this – or perhaps ask a student in your class who you know to be a dancer to demonstrate this.

You could add some percussion rhythm to this, using a tambourine and a drum. The tambourine can play the off beats, i.e. the "&" and the drum the strong beat. See the following musical example.

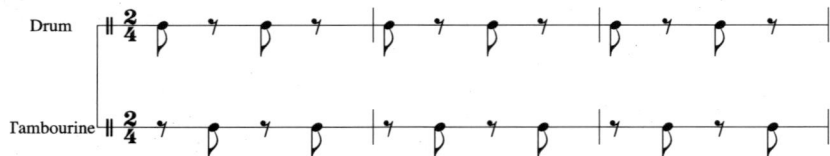

If there is time try playing follow the leader in small groups or work for a time to create an interesting movement pattern using the step.

DAY FOUR

It is wise to review all the previous steps at the beginning of each day.

Now try these four different patterns: A, B, C and D.

A) Using the change feet, change direction, from Day Three, challenge the children to do a half turn on the hop step. If they were moving from right to left before the hop they are now moving from left to right but because of the turn they are still progressing in the same direction around the room (clockwise or counterclockwise) Try this yourself to be able to demonstrate. Have them work in a scatter formation when they are first trying this. If you have little space, do it with a few children at a time.

B) Set 2 lines, perpendicular to the front of the class, each with 5 or 6 students facing forward towards the front of the class. The movement is parallel to the front of the class. The left line will chassée 2 times to the right passing behind the matching person in the right line, while, at the same time, the right line does 2 chassées to the left passing in front of the left line. Return to place doing the pattern that the other line did. (That is: the new left line will pass behind while the new right line passes in front.) See Figure 1 below.

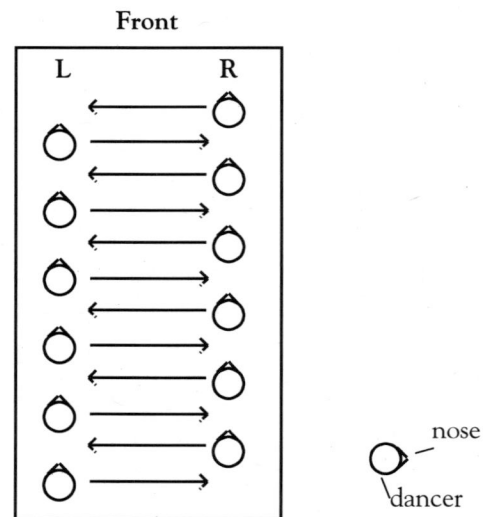

Figure 1

C) The same two lines, but this time the lines face each other and join hands along the line with the people beside them. This time the movement is perpendicular to the front of the class.

Both lines will move in mirror-image. That is, one line travels to the left while the other travels to the right (see Figure 2).

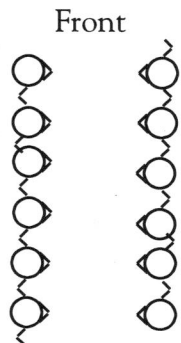

Front

hands joined

Travel sideways toward the front for four chassées.

then

Travel opposite direction four chassées to end in starting place

Figure 2

D) The lines move in opposite directions. That is, they will do identical footwork which makes one move toward the front of the room and the other towards the back. Both lines chassée right and then both lines chassée left (see figure 3).

then

Figure 3

You can add percussion rhythm or melody to back up this movement.

If time permits, ask the children to create their own patterns that incorporate the chassée and the walk or skip of the first classes.

Use the pattern of music suggested here or anything that is in 2/4. When they show you their creations, talk about the musical rhythm and how it helps them decide on the sequence of steps.

I'se the B'y

Traditional arr. Brass

Tip: I would play the alto xylophone part using two sets of players. One to play the chords and the other to play the E D E. As well, note that the last two bars of the bass part need a bit of extra work.

DAY FIVE – A DANCE: THE FLYING SCOTSMAN

This dance was created by Hugh Thurston of Vancouver after a visit to Great Britain and a trip taken on the express train "The Flying Scotsman."

Formation: 2 lines of 4 dancers each. The lines face each other. Leave enough space beside each dancer for another dancer to pass through.

Figure 1: Using 16 skipping steps, and a follow the leader type of line, one line weaves in and out of the other line. The whole line participates: i.e. the front person leads across the top and behind the first person in the other line. Move between persons 1 and 2, then dance in front of person 2, Move between persons 2 and 3, then dance behind person 3. Move between persons 3 and 4 and move straight across to original side, turn and skip up to place. For dancer number 1 this will take 12 skipping steps and 4 to return. For dancer number 2 there is one count to move into place then 12 skipping steps and 3 to return; dancer number 3, 2 counts to move into place, 12 skipping steps and 2 to return and dancer number 4, 3 counts to move into place, 12 skipping steps and one step to return. All dancers end by facing the first line.

The second line now repeats the pattern. Weaving in and out of the people in the first line – also for 16 skipping steps.

Figure 2: The two dancers at the top of each line move toward each other and join 2 hands, and chassée for 8 counts down the center of the lines with the joining of the hands being part of the 8 counts. They reverse direction and chassée back 8 counts, BUT… they will only go as far as the last dancers, release hands and move out to the end of their own line. Again, the release of the hands will be part of the eight counts. All the other dancers, meanwhile are standing still but MUST move up one position when the dancing couple passes them. This will put everyone in a new position ready to continue the dance.

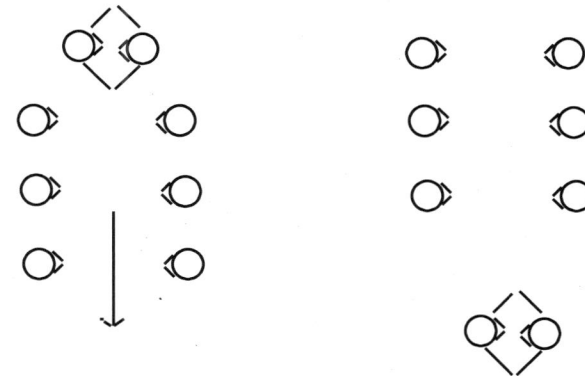

Flying Scotsman, Figure 2

Figure 3: All dancers in each line join hands along the line and will chassée in mirror-image (as in practice Figure 2 above) moving toward the bottom of the room 8 counts and

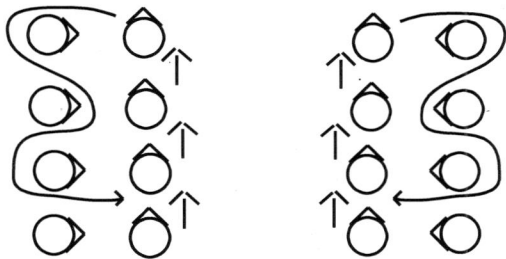

Flying Scotsman, Figure 1

back to place 8 counts. Dance begins again with a new top couple.

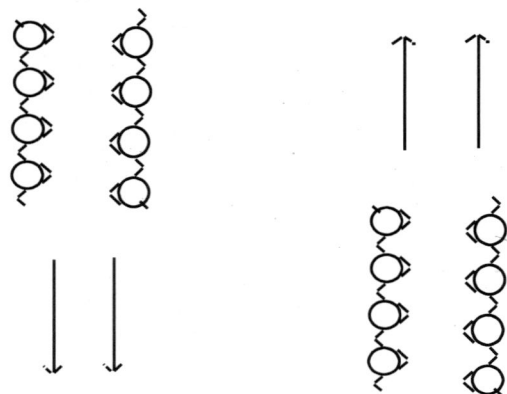

Flying Scotsman, Figure 3

DAY SIX – LEARN THE MUSIC

Learn the music to accompany the dance. I have given you the sample of *I'se the B'y* with a very simple accompaniment to be quickly learned. You can use any music which is 2 beats to the bar either 2/4 or 6/8

The children can sing the melody or it can be played on recorder or one of the melodic instruments. The purpose of this project is the dance so I have made the music simple.

DAY SEVEN

Try the whole thing all together. If the music was easily learned by the whole class, switch the musicians and the dancers so everyone gets a chance to do both parts. In this way they see and hear the integration of the dance and the music – something that Carl Orff thought to be very important.

DAY EIGHT

Day Seven could be the end of this project. However, if you wish to do more movement, you should discuss the different dance forms. The one we learned was in two lines. Some dances are in circles or squares. Demonstrate with some children – chassée around the circle in a group. Demonstrate a dance in a square with one or two students on each side of the square. Demonstrate walking together then walking apart within this square. Demonstrate changing partners across the square. Maybe you want to try a square dance. Ask the students for suggestions of movement with these lines, squares or circles

Let them work in groups to create some movements in a square or a circle using walking, skipping and chassée that uses the music *I'se the B'y*. Or perhaps you have another piece of music suitable for dance that they have already learned.

Give the children ten minutes and see what they create. Some of them will probably amaze you. You could carry this on by joining some of their creations and perhaps coming up with a new dance of their own.

I will stop here but you could carry on with this project becoming more sophisticated as you go. I find the children never tire of creating dances to Orff music. Once you have tried this folk song and given them a bit of the language of dance – i.e.. walk, skip, chassée, forward, backward, right, left, lines, squares, circles – you can ask them to create dances to some of the music in the Orff Schulwerk. There is wonderful dance music in all five volumes.

Exploring the Rhythm of Word Patterns

We often ask children to create a melody based on a given poem or saying.

This project is the opposite – an exercise in making word patterns fit a given rhythm. The final objective is to create a vocal word presentation that sounds like the rhythm in the music on which it is based.

The class can then play the piece of music with all of its parts and then say the word rhythms by themselves and hear how the word rhythms echo the music.

This type of exercise makes children very aware of the rhythm in their speech. Certain words fit only certain rhythm patterns and the emphasis must fall on the right syllable in order to be understood.

When we learn a foreign language it is often the rhythm of the language that we get wrong rather than the words themselves.

Tip: If you have never worked with word rhythms you might want to try the last project in this book, Repeating Rhythms, before you try this one. It could help the students to understand how words work together to make rhythms.

Notes and Inspiration

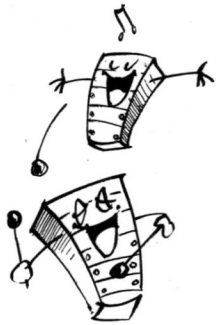

Patterns in Words

Fitness Class is a piece of music which I know works well with this project. But there are many others in the Orff literature. The ideal piece is one with many parts that are rhythmically very different. The music I have chosen has three distinct sections, which allows for different sections to be represented by different word patterns.

Take time to learn the music thoroughly. I have described only three days because my focus here is on the word patterns – it may take more or less time depending on your class and their experience. If your class already knows a piece of suitable music, or you would rather use a composition that is easier to play, then start your word patterns at Day Four. You can apply what I have said here to any piece of music

DAY ONE – LEARN THE MELODY

Learn to play the music on the instruments. This can be done in a similar fashion as the earlier project in this book *The Orff Orchestra*.

I suggest that with *Fitness Class* you start with part B, only because it is a more upbeat part of the piece. The melody starts in the third bar of the B section and bar three to bar six could be sung. To play this I would start with the first two bars after the intro, add to this the next two bars (identical to the first two bars except for the ending) and you have the first four bars of the melody. This gives the children the intro and the melody for the beginning of part B.

The second section of the melody for part B is an exact repeat up a fifth. I have found that once children can play the note patterns in one place, putting them up a fifth causes few problems. The melody then returns down a fifth to end the B section. Of course, as earlier in the book, if you have only ten instruments for thirty children, there will have to be a lot of sharing but it is important that all the children should learn all the parts.

The bass part, easy for those who can keep a steady rhythm, can be played by one child against the melody played by the rest.

DAY TWO – THE OSTINATO FOR PART B AND PART C

The alto xylophone part in part B is easy to play notewise but tricky to sustain the correct rhythm. I find when children are asked to play on the offbeat it is sometimes useful for them to pretend to play in the air for the strong beat and then play the instrument on the weak beat.

Once your children have learned this, try the melody from Day One with this ostinato. Do not be surprised or dismayed if the first time you try this it does not work. You might try the alto xylophone part alone with the bass part so that the children can hear how it fits together. I sometimes play the ostinato offbeat rhythm on a drum along with the children until they can really feel the music.

Now try part C. This is easier to put together. Learn the melody. It is only two bars long. The alto xylophone part is in fact the first four bars of melody on the soprano xylophone part from part B and the bass remains the same. You may well get to try part B and part C by the end of Day Two, or it may take an extra day to make this work.

Fitness Class

Alice Brass

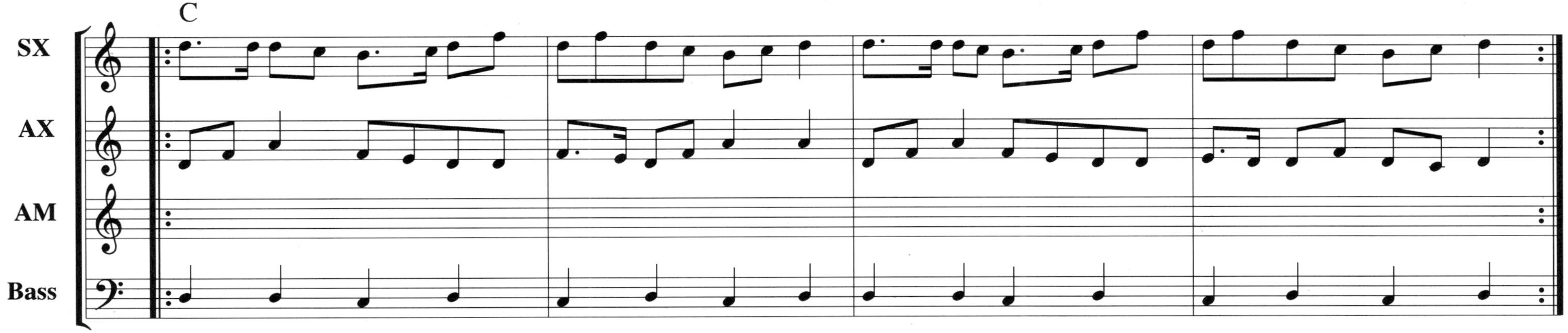
SX
AX
AM
Bass
C

Day Three – Learn part A

Review parts B and C and then learn Part A. It is much slower and more mellow and the melody is played on the metallophones. If you do not have two different metallophones, play one of the parts on a glockenspiel. The bass part here requires a few more notes than in parts B and C.

The drum rhythm for this part is quite difficult to play as a repeating pattern when the other music is being played. You will have to put a least one strong player on this. I find the easiest way to put this together is to break the beat into eight parts and then everyone can hear how their part works

Try the entire piece. There will be some difficulties with the transitions but these can worked out the longer you play the piece. I have always found the class to enjoy this piece and often ask for someone to come to be an audience to hear them play.

If you need more days to learn the piece take them. The children need to feel the rhythms and melodies easily before you start on Day Four.

Day Four – Working out word rhythms

Ask for some suggestions of small thoughts or subjects that would fit the rhythms found in *Fitness Class* and discuss why some work better than others; e.g. schoolwork, classrooms, summer holidays, music groups, zoos, television shows, or if you want integration then some area of history or mathematics you are working on.

With the whole class, talk about the rhythm of the top part of section B. I have given you examples here only so you will see how I expect it to work.

An example: Road Rage

> " *Traf-fic lights, chang-ing quick-ly, Now I'll have to stop here.*" Each syllable has a note and the word "Now" has more emphasis.

If a student suggested "Traf-fic lights red green, Turn-ing ve-ry quick-ly" you could point out that red and green have only one syllable each and while you could sing two different notes on one word we are trying here to be able to say the music so we need a word for each syllable. As well "Turn" before "ing" does not need the emphasis of a dotted quarter note and so the emphasis is wasted.

Ask for may different examples on many different subjects.

Then try the AX ostinato part in the B section. As suggested once at an Orff workshop, I use "sniff" as the place holder for the rest. Carrying on with the idea of traffic I could suggest

Sniff "Honk", Sniff "beep, beep", Sniff "Honk", Sniff, "Honk".

Ask the children for their suggestions. Try two of the word rhythms together so the students can see where you are headed.

Play with this idea for the entire class.

DAY FIVE – CREATING A THREE PART WORD RHYTHM FOR PART B

A word rhythm of the bass part is quite straightforward. It should probably set the theme of the piece. For example with this piece

> *"Road rage, take care"*

Once again ask for student input. This will be easier than on the previous day.

Having reinforced the activities of Day Four, divide the children into groups, three or four to a group, and ask them to come up with three word rhythms, one each for SX, AX and bass of part B, on a central theme that works with this piece. Suggestions for themes as before include classroom activities, playground activities, movies, video games, a story you have just discussed, the mall, holidays, pets or whatever works in your school culture.

Give them ten to twelve minutes then ask to hear their creations. Talk about why they work and which ones are better.

This day could be repeated if the results are not strong enough to use. In the end you will have more than one student saying each rhythm but the important thing is that the rhythms work.

DAY SIX – WORD RHYTHMS FOR PART C AND CHOOSING A THEME

Work with the rhythms of part C of the piece.

An example:

> *"Trucks are always big and noisy*
> *climbing up a long steep hill"*

As noted previously, part C for the alto xylophone is the same as the first four bars of part B on the soprano xylophone. You have a choice. You can use the same word rhythm as the part B or you can create a new one.

Again divide them into groups, perhaps different groups, to create the C section. Give them ten to twelve minutes to be creative and then ask to see their work.

The subjects will still be varied and so after completing these creations you could decide on a theme that seems to work well for both parts.

Henceforth you will work on word patterns that describe only one subject to pull the piece together as a unit.

DAY SEVEN – WORD RHYTHMS FOR PART A

Now you are working with only one theme and it is time to try part A.

The rhythm part for the drums is quite difficult to keep steady. On the same theme as before, "traffic", you could use

> *"Foll-ow-ing, foll-ow-ing, too close"*

The two metallophone parts are quite easy to do.

An example:

> *Alto xylophone: "Slow – – Go"*
> *Soprano xylophone: "Al- ways con-cen trate"*
> *Bass: "Rush-ing home but the lights seem to turn red"*

Repeat the groupings and work time and again ask for samples of their work on this A section.

DAY EIGHT – PUT THE WHOLE PIECE TOGETHER

Try the entire class and the entire piece of music in word rhythm. This is harder than it would first seem and may require some practice; perhaps a leader (you or some student) and perhaps an underlying steady drum beat to keep the words together.

Review the music and try the sequence of music and then word rhythms.

This could be the end unless you want to carry on to a performance.

DAY NINE – ON TO PERFORMANCE

Ask the individual groups to add some simple movement to their speech rhythm. It must be simple but can help to create emphasis to their words.

Now, after you review the music try playing the piece, then saying the rhythm and then playing the piece. You might want to try it the other way around – i.e. say, then play, then say. Ask the children which they like the best.

You might want to create an introduction or a conclusion. You will find this a very effective performance.

Mother Goose Rhymes for the 21st Century

This is an excellent project for exploring meter in poetry and the ideas behind literature. Children often do not know that the poems they chant may have had serious meaning when first written.

> *Pease porridge hot, pease porridge cold,*
> *Pease porridge in the pot nine days old.*

This rhyme refers to the poor way in which children were fed.

This could become

> *Green broccoli hot, green broccoli cold,*
> *Better eat it fast before it grows a mould*

to refer to the recommendations of current nutritionists on the benefits of eating broccoli.

> *Jack be nimble, Jack be quick,*
> *Jack jump over the candlestick*

could become

> *Jack be nimble, Jack be neat,*
> *Jack jump over the compost heap.*

The rhyme about time –

> *Hickory, Dickory Dock, The mouse ran up the clock.*
> *The clock struck one, the mouse ran down,*
> *Hickory, Dickory Dock.*

In our time it could be

> *Hickory, dickory dock; pollution must come to a stop.*
> *The time has come, the damage is done*
> *Hickory, Dickory Dock.*

These are samples of some children's work only to show you what can be created.

Notes and Inspiration

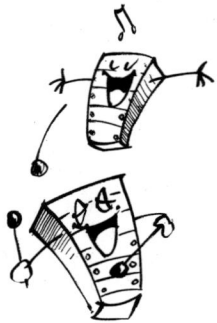

Old Rhymes, New Ideas

DAY ONE – DISCUSS THE NURSERY RHYMES

Talk about the nursery rhymes. Ask for examples and write them down. I would write them down myself and later give them a copy of all of the suggestions. However, if you teach core subjects as well as Orff, then you might want to integrate this into a writing, spelling or poetry class. You do not have to limit this to nursery rhymes but these seem to scan simply and are usually very short and to the point.

This should take at least part of the first day if not all of it. If there is time left, ask for an attempt to turn one of these rhymes into 21st century thoughts. I find it best not to give them too many examples but you could use one of the ideas in the introduction to start.

You will probably get several interesting ideas from the students.

A HISTORICAL NOTE

Hey diddle diddle
The cat and the fiddle
The cow jumped over the moon
The little dog laughed to see such sport
And the dish ran away with the spoon.

Apparently this rhyme was based on the fact that the person who served the meal to the royals was called "the dish," and "the spoon" was the person who tested the food before the royals ate it in case there was poison. It seems that one moonlit night a particular dish did run away with a particular spoon.

DAY TWO – SUGGESTION FOR NEW RHYMES

Working from the copies of the rhymes from Day One, ask for one new verse from each group based on one of the old nursery rhymes or other poems they presented. (Divide the children into groups of two or three. I find bigger groups will argue too much or else some children are simply left out.)

I would allow only about ten minutes for this activity so the children maintain their focus.

Listen to the presentations and then send them off again either to improve their rhymes or make up another. Often children will learn a great deal more from each other's work than anything we can give them.

If time permits listen to these again. After we have created many poems or rhymes I type them out to give out to the next class so that all can work on any poem. The importance is the nursery rhyme quality, and in my project it was the environmental theme. You might rather have another theme or make it more specific, for example, only poems on water use or trash disposal such as

Natasha and John climbed a hill that was long
To fetch a pail of water.
The bugs had fled, the plants were dead
And they were all the sadder.

Run About

Alice Brass

Lyrics: Run a - about, Run a - bout; Find a part - ner or you're out. One Two Three Four Five Six Seven Eight Ni - ne Ten. Here we are to start a - gain.

I have suggested it would take only two days to get here but it might in fact take three or four.

You could end the project here after the creation of the poems and perhaps use them in a science presentation or some other academic way.

I prefer to go on and create games using these rhymes.

Days Three and Four – Creating games using props and toys

Since nursery rhymes are often used as chants for children's games, making up games to go with these new poems works very well here. I add toys to an activity like this – balls, skipping ropes, hula hoops, tossing rings, lummi sticks, ribbons, etc. How you approach this depends on the space you have available and the control of the class. You might want to demonstrate a game like musical chairs. You can start with six children being the chairs, kneeling on one knee and seven children skipping around these chairs. Chant one of the poems as you start the game. When the poem ends they must sit down on the knee of one of the chairs. One will be out. Then take away one chair and try again, and so on. Three times round and then all the chairs collapse seems to make a good presentation, but you may have other ideas.

Discuss different games such as skipping patterns, hopscotch, jumping into hula hoops much the same as musical chairs where there are not enough chairs, piling up rubber rings until they fall down, clapping patterns or any other game that seems to work.

Allow only about 10 minutes for the students to work in groups and come up with ideas and then bring them back to show what they have accomplished.

Ask for input from the class about changes, improvements and general suitability of the movement with the words. Some games will work much better than others and some will work better if modified.

Depending on your class length and noise tolerance you may want to spend another day on this. It took my students three hour-long periods to get this together for performance. While working on this you may want to change groupings, change toys and generally experiment with their ideas.

Day Five – Creating a pattern to join the poems together

When you have some good presentations you can put them all together to make a performance. You need something to join each game with the next one.

This is a sample of a verse that you might use to join the presentations together.

> *Run about, run about, find a partner or you're out*
> *1 2 3 4 5 6 7 8 9 10*
> *Here we are to start again.*

I have suggested an Orff accompaniment for this verse. This is, of course, completely optional.

This type of verse makes a good way to join all the poems together and allows the changing of groups while the performance continues. You might prefer to make your own verse or ask for input from the children

Other joining sections could be rap rhythm, percussion rhythm or simple word ostinato. A recorder player following in the footsteps of the pied piper of Hamelin might also work well.

DAY SIX — THE ENTIRE PERFORMANCE

We are calling this Day Six but it might be Day Eight or Nine depending on how much time you have taken with Day Three and Day Four.

Put the whole thing together – poems, joining verses, movement, etc. If you want the children to be in more than one activity, you have to design a way to move them around. I always try to have every child play instruments for part of the performance and run, dance, play, and act for another part. This is more fun but not necessary if you do not have time to arrange it.

If you want to perform this, it will take many more days in order to position the various movement activities so they can all be seen.

In my experience this activity is great fun and enjoyed by all participants and the audience.

Rhythmic Repetition

Incessant rhythm is a big feature of today's music for young people. Note how many of the most popular sellers are rap presentations.

Experimenting with various rhythms played together seems to attract the children's attention. Once the beat is secure, many amazing rhythms can be performed ensemble. Many of these rhythms would be very hard to notate or read but learned completely by ear they seem easy and fun. Currently, "Stomp" is a group which performs this type of repetitive rhythm in sound and movement. Videos of this group do exist and make a good starting place. Word rhythms work well here; the subject must be very clear and

the ideas very cohesive. The result will be a strong repetitive rhythmic performance.

This is a very short project and probably more suitable for grade five and up but you will find it a lot of fun and see active participation from some children who are normally unwilling to play solo roles.

Notes and Inspiration

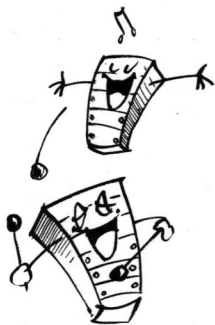

Repeating Rhythms

DAY ONE – INTRODUCE THE IDEA

If possible watch a video of "Stomp" or some other similar performance. Talk about what makes the performance effective.

Ask for a suggestion of an underlying beat and have some students clap this over and over.

Example: clap rest, clap rest, etc.

Now ask for another rhythm to go with this. This is similar to the project on poetry in this book but without the poem for structure. Have another group of children try this along with the first group with the clapping pattern.

Example: stamp, stamp, stamp, rest – still using only single undivided beats.

A third pattern could be a patching pattern

Example: patsch-ing, patsch- ing, patsch-ing, rest where the notation would be titi titi titi rest

Have a third group perform this along with the other two groups. These rhythms are very basic but the children will get the idea.

If there is time, try this again with different rhythms perhaps more complicated with input from the children but still directed by you.

DAY TWO – CREATING REPEATING RHYTHMS

Divide the children into groups and have them create their own combination of rhythms. I suggest between three and six children in each group but you know your own class.

Give them ten minutes to create some repeating rhythms. Let the class see and hear these and discuss them.

Where's the wait - er, Where's the wait - er,

Soup is cold!, Soup is cold!

Please, bring some wa - ter, Please, bring some wa - ter.

Hur - ry, Hur - ry, Must be home by nine; Hu - ry, Hur - ry, Must be home by nine.

Now discuss a central idea that could be used in words to create a repeating rhythm.

Example: Eating in a restaurant:

- *Where's the waiter, where's the waiter*
- *Soup is cold, soup is cold*
- *Please bring some water, please bring some water*
- *Hurry, hurry, Must be home by nine; hurry, hurry, Must be home by nine*

Try this or something similar with the class.

Discuss how the words must be said to make the rhythm work.

In this example, if the basic rhythm, "Where's the waiter" is straight ta, ta, ta, ta then the second line, "Soup is cold" would be ta, ta, ta, rest and the last line would have to be said as titi, titi, tafitifi, ta. Also note that in this example every part starts on beat one. If the word "the" was added to "Soup is cold", it would have to be phrased as a pickup to be said as it would be spoken normally.

DAY THREE – SELECTING AND DEVELOPING ONE IDEA

Ask the class to use word thoughts to describe a central idea – i.e. sports games, school work, musical events, competitions, tests and exams, or anything else they think of. Depending on your class it may be necessary to discuss some of these ideas before they start on their own creations.

In groups of three to six have them develop their ideas as we did as a class on the day before.

From my experience you will be quite delighted with their creations. This seems to fit easily into their current culture.

DAY FOUR – ADDING PERCUSSION AND MOVEMENT

Add one percussion instrument to each group's performance. This could be a drum, the side of a desk, a set of keys, etc. An incessant regular beat can be played under the repeated words of each person. The important thing is that there is no pause.

Some speakers can speak together, others can follow. Alternatively, one person can start, then two together, then three, etc. The difficulty here is that sometimes you cannot hear the third or fourth idea. You might prefer to set out each individual thought by itself and then add them one by one, or perhaps two by two and only all together.

This exercise is great fun for children and they often can add small bits of movement – turning from side to side, stepping up and down from a box or bench, rap type dancing – anything that helps the rhythm to continue and to tell the story.

Having worked on a unit like this I find the children using the technique in other presentations. It showed up when we were working on making machines and other teachers say that it shows up in drama improvisations.

Closing

These ideas on exploration are to encourage you to further explore the arts through Orff with its simplicity and wonderful sound. Accomplished musicians and beginners alike enjoy the Orff approach. They can create something which belongs to them.

As I said in my first book, *Orff Day by Day*, let the children's ingenuity and creativity lead you through these projects. Make certain that the children have enough basic skills to create what you are asking and then let their ideas lead you.

All of the arts have value in children's lives and the more we discover about the developing brain the more we realize this.

This type of Orff exploration gives you a chance to introduce the children to areas of the arts they might otherwise never enter.

If some project does not work exactly as you expect or hope, persevere and start again. I have often said to my class that something did not work too well, perhaps because of my directions, and we should start afresh. The pleasure they get from their final results is worth all the effort to get them there.

Appendices

Glossary

CANON: A composition in which one part is imitated strictly in another part at any pitch or time interval. The imitation starts after the part to be imitated has been heard.

ECHO CLAPPING: The clapping, snapping, stamping, etc. of patterns performed first by the leader then by the group.

FOUND SOUNDS: Sounds made using everyday materials like door keys, paper, music stands, pencils on desks, etc.

IMPROVISATION: The act of rendering music or body movement with little or no preparation.

MIRRORING: Actions in body movement or body percussion such as clapping, snapping, etc. where one person reflects exactly and simultaneously the movement of another.

OSTINATO: A repeated musical figure played as an accompaniment to a melody or song.

PATSCHEN: Patting the right hand on the right knee and the left hand on the left knee usually simultaneously.

PENTATONIC SCALE: A five-tone normally whole-tone scale which omits the fourth and seventh tones of the major scale. It can be built on the tonic of the major scale, and thus C pentatonic is CDE GA, or it can be built on the sub-mediant of the major scale and be A CDE G.

QUESTION AND ANSWER: The execution of a phrase of melody and/or rhythm which seems to ask a question by not ending on the tonic, followed by a similar answering phrase usually ending on the tonic or a strong beat.

RONDO: A musical form resulting from alternating the main theme or A section with other contrasting sections. The A section is repeated between each entry of another section. For example: ABACADA.

ROUND: A "circle canon", that is, a canon in which the melody is repeated at the same pitch level.

TIMBRE: Tone color or the difference between tones of the same pitch produced by different instruments.

CURRICULUM GUIDELINES

It is often necessary to justify a program such as Orff in terms of a stated curriculum. The following is an outline of how a program following some of the ideas in this book could suit a particular curriculum. Educational curricula are often changing but the basic outline usually remains.

The main focus of this book is exploration of the arts through rhythm, dance, drama and art. The first book, *Orff Day by Day*, deals with specific skill development, including improvisation, lummi sticks, canon, and adapting poetry. This book builds on those skills to explore rhythm, dance, shape and color and the language in general.

Several of the projects in this book deal with rhythm, beat and the way these occur in everyday language as well as in poetry. In speaking the language, children are often unaware of the importance of rhythm, both in how they pronounce the words and how they shape their sentences. This becomes even more important when learning a foreign language.

Poetry is often expressed rhythmically and working out beats and ostinatos to accompany a poem certainly helps in committing this poem to memory if that is desirable.

Reading symbols and reacting to them by playing an instrument is very easy for some children, but can be difficult for others, especially the younger ones. Some of the Orff techniques are very useful in this regard.

In the project on shapes and color the children are learning to interpret visual objects in terms of sound. This is very important in the current arts culture. The use of the different timbres of the Orff instruments created to accompany the designs allows discussion of tone colors and how they work best together.

The co-operation needed when playing in an ensemble is necessary for the Orff orchestra. The requires listening skills and concentration for the whole group to stay together.

The two projects requiring footwork are quite different in focus. One uses the feet to describe dramatic subjects and can be enhanced with sound effects. This can be accompanied by a discussion of the importance of body language in drama and dance.

The project on the folk dance, on the other hand, is a beginning to teaching children about folk dance, its origins and its music. Teaching a folk dance can often accompany a history, geography or social studies class. The steps are very simple and require some simple technique.

The study of nursery rhymes is a good look at the history of children's play and an interesting way to compare today's climate of play and politics.

All of these projects show how music can be used as a means of communication to discuss many aspects of our culture.

There are no doubt many other ways that Orff activities meet the requirements of a curriculum. I have included these few to explain that while Orff may seem merely to be playing with the children, a lot of integrated music education is taking place in a very happy surrounding.

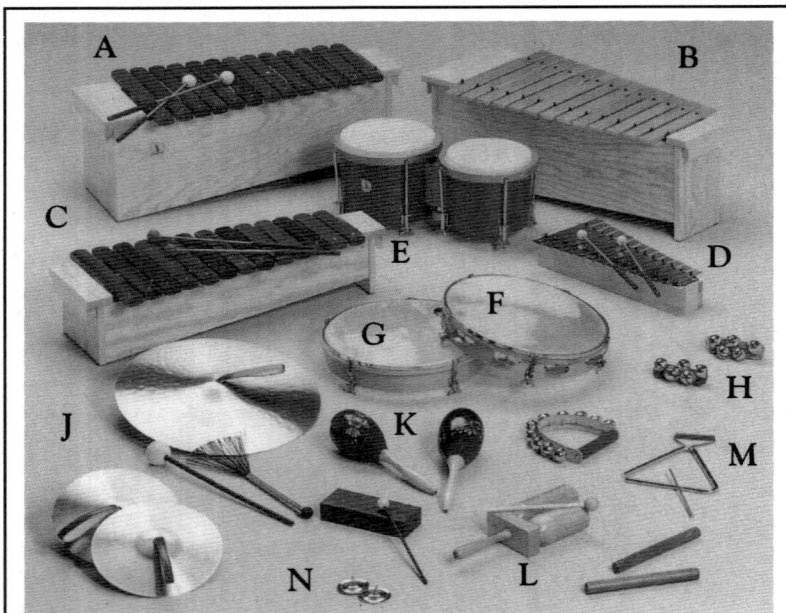

Courtesy Studio 49/ Waterloo Music

A SELECTION OF ORFF INSTRUMENTS

A – Alto Xylophone
B – Alto Metallophone
C – Soprano Xylophone
D – Alto Glockenspiel
E – Bongo Drums
F – Tambourine
G – Hand Drum

H – Bells
J – Cymbals
K – Maracas
L – Wood Blocks and Claves
M – Triangle
N – Finger Cymbals

Where to get more information

If you like the ideas in this book and would like to know more about Orff and the Orff approach to learning, you can attend Orff workshops, conferences and Orff courses. Many music publishers have displays at these conferences and workshops where you can purchase books and equipment to enhance your teaching. As well, this is often a place to make contacts and friends who will help you further with your program. To find out where and when these are taking place you can contact the following organizations:

In Canada: Carl Orff Canada, www.orffcanada.ca

In the U.S.A: American Orff-Schulwerk Association, www.aosa.org

Also by Alice Brass – *Orff Day by Day*

In this companion volume to *Orff Explorations*, Alice Brass introduces ideas on improvisation, canon, rondo, lummi sticks and the use of poetry with nine Orff projects. This clear step-by-step approach has helped many teachers bring the spirit of the Orff approach to their classroom activities.

ISBN 978-1-896941-02-8, $20.00